Celebrations in My World

Kwanzaa

Crabtree Publishing Company

www.crabtreebooks.com

W9-AVJ-254

Crabtree Publishing Company

www.crabtreebooks.com

Author: Molly Aloian
Coordinating editor: Chester Fisher
Series editor: Susan Labella
Project manager: Kavita Lad (Q2AMEDIA)
Art direction: Dibakar Acharjee (Q2AMEDIA)
Cover design: Ranjan Singh (Q2AMEDIA)
Design: Tarang Saggar (Q2AMEDIA)
Photo research: Sakshi Saluja (Q2AMEDIA)
Editor: Kelley MacAulay
Copy editor: Molly Aloian
Proofreader: Reagan Miller
Project coordinator: Robert Walker
Production coordinator: Katherine Kantor
Font management: Mike Golka
Prepress technicians: Samara Parent, Ken Wright

Photographs:
Cover: Corbis/Jupiter Images; Title
page: Mark Adams/Getty Images;
P5: The Image Works/Topfoto; P7:
The Image Works/Topfoto; P9: Corbis/
Jupiter Images; P10: David Young-Wolff/
Alamy; P11: Topham Picturepoint;
P12-13: Sergey I/Shutterstock; P15:
Sean Locke/Istockphoto; P17: Brand X
Pictures/Jupiter Images; P18: Liquidlibrary/
Jupiter Images; P19: Liquidlibrary/Jupiter
Images; P20: Temelko Temelkov/
Istockphoto; P21: The Image Works/
Topfoto; P23: The Image Works/
Topfoto; P25: Comstock Images/
Jupiter Images; P26: Photoeuphoria/
Dreamstime; P27: Undergroundarts.co.uk/
Shutterstock; P28(tr): Lucian Coman/
Shutterstock; P28(bl): Associated Press;
P29: Juburg/Shutterstock; P31: Blend
Images/Jupiter Images

Library and Archives Canada Cataloguing in Publication

Aloian, Molly
    Kwanzaa / Molly Aloian.

(Celebrations in my world)
Includes index.

ISBN 978-0-7787-4284-5 (bound).--ISBN 978-0-7787-4302-6 (pbk.)

    1. Kwanzaa--Juvenile literature. I. Title. II. Series.

GT4403A46 2008   j394.2612   C2008-903114-8

Library of Congress Cataloging-in-Publication Data

Aloian, Molly.
    Kwanzaa / Molly Aloian.
        p. cm. -- (Celebrations in my world)
    Includes index.
    ISBN-13: 978-0-7787-4302-6 (pbk. : alk. paper)
    ISBN-10: 0-7787-4302-0 (pbk. : alk. paper)
    ISBN-13: 978-0-7787-4284-5 (reinforced library binding : alk. paper)
    ISBN-10: 0-7787-4284-9 (reinforced library binding : alk. paper)
    1. Kwanzaa--Juvenile literature. 2. African Americans--Social life and
customs--Juvenile literature. I. Title. II. Series.

GT4403.A45 2008
394.2612--dc22
                                                                2008021206

Crabtree Publishing Company

www.crabtreebooks.com   1-800-387-7650

Published in Canada
Crabtree Publishing
616 Welland Ave.
St. Catharines, ON
L2M 5V6

Published in the United States
Crabtree Publishing
PMB16A
350 Fifth Ave., Suite 3308
New York, NY 10118

Published in the United Kingdom
Crabtree Publishing
White Cross Mills
High Town, Lancaster
LA1 4XS

Published in Australia
Crabtree Publishing
386 Mt. Alexander Rd.
Ascot Vale (Melbourne)
VIC 3032

Contents

What Is Kwanzaa?

Kwanzaa is an African-American holiday. Each year, millions of people celebrate Kwanzaa for seven days, from December 26 to January 1. People celebrate with their families, friends, and others in their **communities**. A community is a group of people who live together in an area. While celebrating Kwanzaa, people eat delicious foods, wear special clothes, sing, dance, and celebrate their **ancestors**.

DID YOU KNOW?

Swahili is a language spoken in parts of Africa. The word "Kwanzaa" comes from the Swahili word "kwanza." The word "kwanza" means "first."

This family is getting ready to celebrate Kwanzaa. They will sing, dance, share food, and remember their traditions.

How It Began

Kwanzaa was created in 1966 by a teacher named Dr. Maulana Ron Karenga. Dr. Karenga's idea for Kwanzaa came from first-fruit festivals that take place in Africa. During first-fruit festivals, African people come together to celebrate the harvest. They give thanks for the crops they grew and for what they had achieved by working together. Kwanzaa is a time for African-Americans to think about what they can achieve by working together.

DID YOU KNOW?

Many first-fruit festivals in Africa were held for seven-days at the end of December, just like Kwanzaa.

For hundreds of years, African-Americans were forced to be slaves. By working together, however, they gained freedom and achieved equal rights. Kwanzaa is a time for African-Americans to learn about their history in America and to celebrate their **cultures** from Africa.

Today, Dr. Karenga, shown far right, teaches students about African-American history at California State University.

Kwanzaa Principles

The number seven is an important part of Kwanzaa. Kwanzaa lasts for seven days. There are seven **principles**, or main beliefs, celebrated during Kwanzaa. The seven principles are unity, self-determination, working together, co-operative economics, purpose, creativity, and faith. Dr. Karenga chose these principles after learning about African cultures. He knew these beliefs had always been important to many African people and he wanted people to think about them.

DID YOU KNOW?

Some people write out the seven principles on a sheet of paper and hang it on a wall during Kwanzaa.

Each of the seven days of Kwanzaa is **dedicated** to one of the principles. To celebrate a principle each day, a family lights one candle.

Children look forward to lighting the candles during Kwanzaa each year.

Kwanzaa Symbols

There are seven **symbols** for Kwanzaa. A symbol is something that stands for something else. The symbols for Kwanzaa are the unity cup, the candle holder, crops (fruits and vegetables), seven candles, a woven mat, corn, and gifts. The symbols are used during different parts of the Kwanzaa celebration.

People display Kwanzaa symbols for the holiday.

DID YOU KNOW?

The **bendera** (behn-deh-rah) is another Kwanzaa symbol. It is a flag. African leader Marcus Garvey created the bendera.

Marcus Garvey, an African leader, created the bendera.

People gather together the seven symbols of Kwanzaa and display them in their homes. Turn the page to learn more about the Kwanzaa symbols.

What They Mean

Each of the Kwanzaa symbols stands for something important in the lives of African-Americans. The unity cup stands for staying together. In fact, another word for unity is togetherness. The candle holder stands for the ancestors who lived in Africa long ago. The Swahili word for candle holder is **kinara**. The kinara is made of wood. It stands in the middle of a Kwanzaa display.

Fruits and vegetables stand for the first African harvest celebrations and the hard work it took Africans to grow the crops. Seven candles stand for Kwanzaa's seven principles. The woven mat stands for tradition and history. People place all the symbols on the mat. Each ear of corn stands for each child in a family. Each kernel represents children that will be born in the future. The final symbol is gifts. Gifts stand for promises made during Kwanzaa that are kept throughout the year.

Getting Ready!

People prepare for Kwanzaa as a family. They place Kwanzaa decorations of black, red, and green, around their homes. They gather the Kwanzaa symbols. The family chooses a unity cup of wood or metal. They make or buy gifts and a candle holder. They arrange colorful fruits and vegetables in baskets. When all of the symbols have been gathered, the family places them together on the woven mat. People also get ready for Kwanzaa by making or buying colorful African clothing to wear.

DID YOU KNOW?

People make foods after celebrating each day. They use squash, bananas, and lamb.

All family members, including children, usually help prepare foods for Kwanzaa. Many families prepare traditional recipes.

Seven Candles

An important part of preparing for Kwanzaa is gathering seven candles to place in the kinara. Three candles are red, three are green, and one is black. The three red candles go on the left side of the kinara. These candles stand for the people's struggles.

The three green candles go on the right side. These stand for a good future. The black candle in the middle stands for African and African-American people. The family lights one candle on each of the seven days of Kwanzaa.

DID YOU KNOW?

The colors of the seven candles are the same as the colors of the bendera.

The kinara can be of many different shapes.

Unity

On the first day of Kwanzaa, family and friends gather together and light the black candle. On this day, they celebrate the principle of unity. After lighting the candle, everyone takes a drink from the unity cup. Unity and togetherness mean different things to different people.

● This girl is drinking from the unity cup.

DID YOU KNOW?

People may give one another gifts during the seven days of Kwanzaa. Gifts may include books by African-American authors and hand made items.

Family members share their thoughts about what unity means. Families celebrate unity by sharing their love and enjoying close friendships. They promise to keep their communities strong by working together. At the end of the celebration, the candle is put out.

The child who lights the candle usually talks first about what unity means to him or her.

Self-Determination

On the second day of Kwanzaa, the family re-lights the black candle and then lights the first red candle. Family members and friends drink from the unity cup and talk about self-determination. Self-determination means having confidence in one's own self. People promise to think and speak for themselves. Some people might perform a skit to show others who they are or who they hope to become. Others teach children how to beat African music on drums. This gives children confidence and connects them to their ancestors' traditions. After the celebration, family and friends usually have a meal together.

● Some children learn to play African drums such as the one shown above.

Music is often an important part of a Kwanzaa celebration.

Working Together

The principle for the third day of Kwanzaa is working together. On this day, the family re-lights the black and red candle. Then they light the first green candle. Do you remember what the color green represents? The future!

On the third day, family and friends drink from the unity cup. They talk about **collective responsibility**. This means working together to solve problems. Many families spend this day working together at household chores.

DID YOU KNOW?

Having a potluck dinner is one way to work together during Kwanzaa. Each person makes a dish to bring to another's home and share with everyone.

Working together and being responsible for each other are important ideas on the third day of Kwanzaa.

Sharing Wealth

On day four, the family re-lights the candles for the first three days of Kwanzaa, as well as another red candle. They drink from the unity cup to celebrate co-operative economics. Co-operative economics is using your own **wealth**, or money and possessions, to help others. People work to help other African-Americans in their neighborhoods. They may promise to shop at stores that African-American people own.

DID YOU KNOW?

The greeting for each day of Kwanzaa is "Habari gani?" which means "What's the news?" in Swahili. The response to the greeting is the principle for that day.

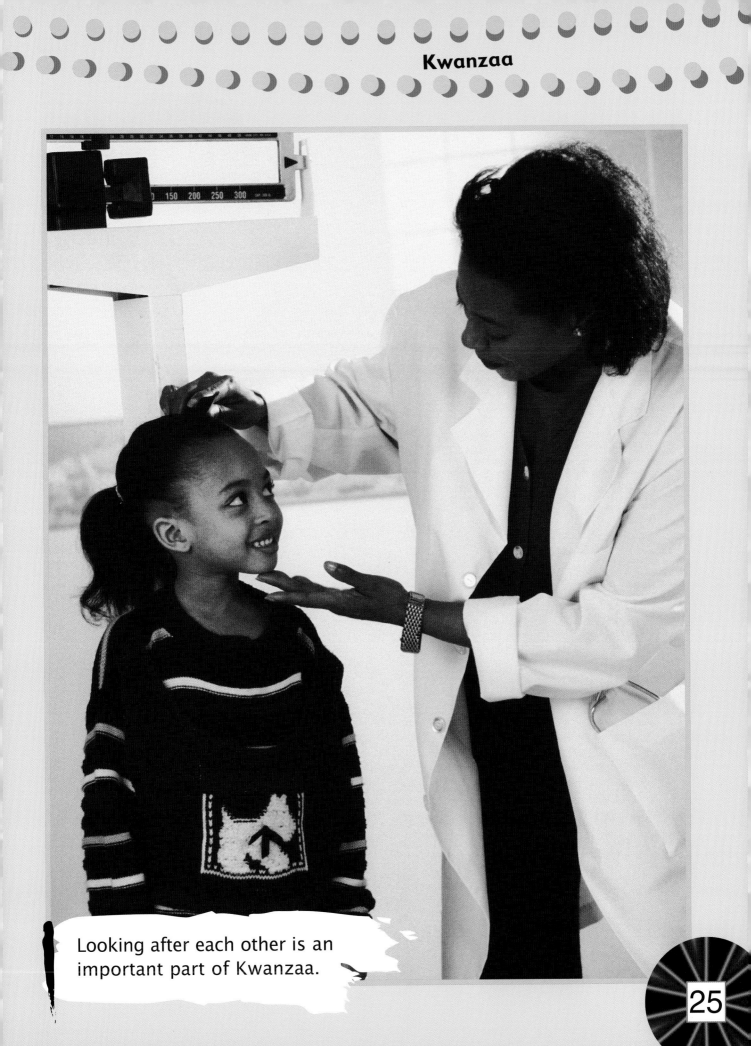

Looking after each other is an important part of Kwanzaa.

Purpose

Purpose is the fifth Kwanzaa principle. On the fifth day, the family drinks from the unity cup before lighting the candles from the first four days, as well as another green candle. They talk about having purpose. Having purpose means accomplishing things and living in a way that is useful to others.

This girl's goal for the following year is to learn how to play the guitar.

People talk about the **goals** they want to reach in the next year. They promise to respect others and themselves. They agree to learn more about African-American values. People tell African-American **folktales** or sing African-American freedom songs. These remind families of great African-Americans who once lived. A fun goal to reach for the fifth day of Kwanzaa is to make home made gifts for others. Some people might cook food and give it to others as gifts. Other people might decorate bottles and fill them with homemade spicy vinegar.

● Someone's goal for the year may be to make jars of foods such as these for gifts.

27

Creativity

Creativity is the sixth principle. The Swahili word for creativity is **kuumba**. Having creativity means using your imagination to make new and original things. On the sixth night of Kwanzaa, people light the first five candles and the third red candle. They express creativity by making up dances that tell stories about African history. People also play African instruments, tell stories, and sing songs.

DID YOU KNOW?

In 1997, the United States Postal Service issued the first Kwanzaa stamp. In 2004, an artist named Daniel Minter created a second Kwanzaa stamp.

They might create art projects such as African masks, **sculptures**, or drawings. They talk about how they can use their creativity to make their communities strong.

Artists use their creativity to make original works of art.

Faith

On the seventh day of Kwanzaa, all of the candles are lit, including the final green candle. The seventh principle is faith. Having faith is to believe and trust. The last day of Kwanzaa is for **reflection**, or quiet thinking. The family members drink from the unity cup and reflect on the faith they have in themselves. They reflect on the faith they have in their family and in their African **heritage**. Children and adults explain what faith means to them.

DID YOU KNOW?

During Kwanzaa celebrations, a man might wear a robe called a kanzu (kahn-zoo). A woman might wear an elegant robe or gown called a bui-bui (booee-booee).

They promise to believe in themselves, in their families and friends, in their African heritage.

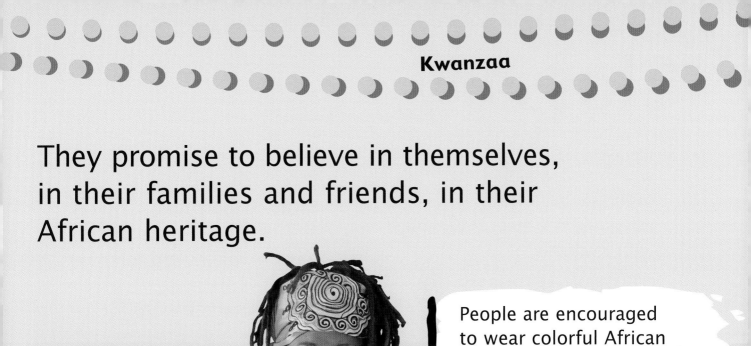

People are encouraged to wear colorful African clothes during Kwanzaa.

31

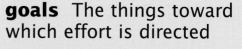

Glossary

ancestors The people from whom an individual or group is descended

bendera The flag associated with Kwanzaa

collective responsibility Working together to solve problems

communities Groups of people who live together in certain areas

culture The beliefs, social practices, and physical characteristics of a group of people

dedicated To set apart for some purpose

folktale A story that is made up

goals The things toward which effort is directed

heritage Something acquired from the past

kinara Swahili word for candle holder

kuumba Swahili word for creativity

principles Main beliefs

reflection Quiet thinking

sculptures Art made by cutting, carving, or molding

Swahili A language spoken in different parts of Africa

symbols Something that stands for something else

wealth A great amount of money

Index

32

Printed in the U.S.A.